copyright©

Mind Over Private Matters
Relapse History & Prevention Plan

Text Copyright©2025; USA Version:2025
By Andrew Hunter Beavers

All Rights Reserved. Printed in the United States of America.

ISBN
Hardcover: 978-1-967616-47-3
Paperback: 978-1-967616-46-6

Andrew Hunter Beavers Books
628 West Broadway STE 300
North Little Rock, Arkansas 72114

Bulk discount available. Contact AB (479-200-2530)

This workbook is to be used in conjunction with individual therapy for substance use and mental health disorders by qualified staf. Each Client participating must have a copy of the workbook journal and may purchase as many as needed for efective Inpatient or Outpatient treatment. Photocopies are prohibited. The target population is substance use, mental health disorders, and individuals introduced to cognitive behavioral therapy (CBT) techniques, including Behavioral Experimentation, to challenge negative and unwanted thought patterns or production. The program may assign the written material of each session as homework. The homework should be completed before an individual session. The workbook journal is not for Group Therapy or full disclosure in a group setting of multiple participants.

Introduction and Purpose

DO SOMETHING DIFFERENT

Cognitive Behavioral Therapy (CBT) is a form of psychotherapy that assists individuals in identifying and modifying detrimental thought patterns and behaviors. This therapeutic approach is frequently employed to address conditions such as anxiety, depression, and various other mental health disorders. The fundamental objective of CBT is to disrupt the cycle of negative thinking, facilitate change, and create thoughts with more positive and constructive alternatives.

Change is an inherent aspect of existence. It is not possible for an individual to remain static while altering their circumstances. Every living organism must undergo processes of change or growth. This principle applies not only to individual human beings but also to couples, teams, organizations, and entire societies. What distinguishes change within the growth process from other processes? Change entails the relinquishment of the old and the facilitation of the emergence of something new. Consequently, one does not return to the original state; rather, the final outcome is either significantly or entirely different from the initial conditions.

What stage of recovery am I?

Healthcare professionals utilize a model that aids in understanding patients' thoughts and emotions regarding behavioral change. By identifying the specific stage at which a patient is operating, the healthcare practitioner can communicate effectively, ensuring alignment in their interaction while avoiding any tendency to push or offend the individual participant.

a. Precontemplation Stage: I don't have a problem with alcohol/drugs. I might need to change, but I don't know if I am ready to change.

b. Preparation Stage: I have planned to change. I must do something about my problem.

c. Action Stage: You start working on a plan to change. You become open-minded and willing to be honest with yourself and others.

d. Maintenance Stage: You have to keep your focus on the progress you are making and your new behavior and practice the principles you are learning in the program. You have a sponsor with whom you stay in close contact, work all the steps, and attend recovery meetings.

RELAPSE PREVENTION QUESTIONNAIRE

Complete the following questionnaire, give your Clinician or Peer Specialist a copy, and keep a copy for the file.

1. How would you define "relapse" in your own words?
   a. _____
   b. _____

2. Identify your triggers and areas for improvement. Create a plan to manage them for your personal growth.
   a. _____
   b. _____
   c. _____

3. What are obsessive thoughts? How do they affect "relapse?".
   a. _____
   b. _____
   c. _____

4. What is the definition of a craving?
   a. _____
   b. _____

5. What do you do when you have a craving?
   a. _____
   b. _____

6. What are some common emotional states or indicators individuals experience as they prepare to relapse?
   a. _____
   b. _____
   c. _____

7. Understanding these signs is crucial for effective intervention and support. How do you handle these feelings or signs?
   a. _____
   b. _____
   c. _____

8. What is a support system?

    _____

    Do you have a sponsor?   YES _____ NO _____

    How often do you regularly attend AA/NA meetings?

    _____

    Please elaborate on your established support systems and describe how
    they contribute to your overall support.

    _____
    _____
    _____
    _____

9. What activities inspire joy and fulfillment in your life?

    _____
    _____

    Why is taking time for yourself important? It helps you recharge and
    improves your focus at work. What do you do?

    _____
    _____
    _____

10. What is your recovery or relapse prevention plan?

    _____
    _____
    _____
    _____
    _____
    _____

RELAPSE HISTORY/PREVENTION

"Am I truly finding the fulfillment and happiness I seek in my life?"

1. Do you have a problem with alcohol and/or drugs?   YES _____ NO _____

2. List 5 reasons you believe you have a problem:

   a. _____
   b. _____
   c. _____
   d. _____
   e. _____

3. Have you ever been in treatment for alcohol/drug use? YES _____ NO _____

   If yes, how many times?

   _____

4. Please enumerate each treatment attempt, specifying the location. duration of stay (completed or incomplete), the outcomes, and key lessons learned. Additionally, Indicate the length of time you maintained sobriety after each attempt and the factors that contributed to subsequent relapses.

   a. _____
   _____
   _____
   _____
   _____
   _____
   _____
   _____
   _____
   _____
   _____

A

b. _____

c. _____

5. List the three people you are most angry at and explain why.

6. List the three people you hold blameless and explain why.

7. Honestly state your three biggest fears.

_____
_____
_____
_____
_____
_____
_____
_____
_____

8. What is the thing that has brought the most guilt to your life?

_____
_____
_____
_____
_____
_____
_____
_____

9. What is the worst thing you have done that brings shame to your life?

_____
_____
_____
_____
_____
_____
_____
_____

10. Have you ever had a sponsor? Yes _____ No _____ If yes, how long?

_____
_____
_____
_____
_____
_____
_____
_____

11. How often did you talk with your sponsor?

_____
_____
_____
_____

12. How many 12-step Meetings did you attend in a week?

_____
_____
_____
_____

13. List 5 character defects you have.

_____
_____
_____
_____
_____
_____
_____
_____

14. List 5 shortcomings you possess.

_____
_____
_____
_____
_____
_____
_____
_____

15. List 5 strengths you possess.

_____
_____
_____
_____
_____
_____
_____
_____

16. List the 5 most important things in your life, listing them in order of importance, and then put a check by the ones you are willing to give up.

_____
_____
_____
_____
_____
_____
_____

17. List 5 of your biggest triggers and a plan to deal with each one.

1._____
_____
_____
_____
_____

2._____
_____
_____
_____
_____

3._____
_____
_____
_____
_____

4._____
_____
_____
_____
_____

5._____
_____
_____
_____
_____

18.   Write your life story (at least eight (5) full pages).

———————————————————————

———————————————————————

———————————————————————

———————————————————————

———————————————————————

———————————————————————

———————————————————————

———————————————————————

———————————————————————

———————————————————————

———————————————————————

———————————————————————

———————————————————————

———————————————————————

———————————————————————

———————————————————————

Date: _____

Welcome to the Michigan Alcohol Screening Test (MAST), Revised

1. Do you feel you are a normal drinker? ("normal" - drink as much or less than most other People)?

    ○ Yes
    ○ No

2. Have you ever awakened the morning after some drinking the night before and found that you could not remember a part of the evening?

    ○ Yes
    ○ No

3. Does any near relative or close friend ever worry or complain about your drinking?

    ○ Yes
    ○ No

4. Can you stop drinking without difficulty after one or two drinks?

    ○ Yes
    ○ No

5. Do you ever feel guilty about your drinking?

    ○ Yes
    ○ No

6. Have you ever attended a meeting of Alcoholics Anonymous (AA)?

    ○ Yes
    ○ No

7. Have you ever gotten into physical fights when drinking?

    ○ Yes
    ○ No

8. Has drinking ever created problems between you and a near relative or close friend?

   ○ Yes
   ○ No

9. Has any family member or close friend gone to anyone for help about your

   ○ Yes
   ○ No

10. Have you ever lost friends because of your drinking?

    ○ Yes
    ○ No

11. Have you ever gotten into trouble at work because of drinking?

    ○ Yes
    ○ No

12. Have you ever lost a job because of drinking?

    ○ Yes
    ○ No

13. Have you ever neglected your obligations, your family, or your work for two or

    ○ Yes
    ○ No

14. Do you drink before noon fairly often?

    ○ Yes
    ○ No

15. Have you ever been told you have liver trouble such as cirrhosis?

    ○ Yes
    ○ No

16. After heavy drinking have you ever had delirium tremens (D.T.'s), severe shaking, visual or auditory (hearing) hallucinations?

    ○ Yes
    ○ No

17. Have you ever gone to anyone for help about your drinking?

    ○ Yes
    ○ No

18. Have you ever been hospitalized because of drinking?

    ○ Yes
    ○ No

19. Has your drinking ever resulted in your being hospitalized in a psychiatric ward?

    ○ Yes
    ○ No

20. Have you ever gone to any doctor, social worker, clergyman or mental health clinic for help with any emotional problem in which drinking was part of the problem?

    ○ Yes
    ○ No

21. Have you been arrested more than once for driving under the influence of alcohol?

    ○ Yes
    ○ No

22. Have you ever been arrested, even for a few hours, because of other behavior while drinking?

    ○ Yes
    ○ No

Date : _____

Welcome to the Drug Abuse Screening Test (DAST)

1. Have you used drugs other than those required for medical reasons?

    ○ Yes
    ○ No

2. Have you abused prescription drugs?

    ○ Yes
    ○ No

3. Do you abuse more than one drug at a time?

    ○ Yes
    ○ No

4. Can you get through the week without using drugs?

    ○ Yes
    ○ No

5. Are you always able to stop using drugs when you want to?

    ○ Yes
    ○ No

6. Have you had "blackouts" or "flashbacks" as a result of drug use?

    ○ Yes
    ○ No

7. Do you ever feel bad or guilty about your drug use?

    ○ Yes
    ○ No

8. Does your spouse (or parents) ever complain about your
    involvement with drugs?

    ○ Yes
    ○ No

9. Has drug abuse created problems between you and your spouse or your
    parents?

    ○ Yes
    ○ No

10. Have you ever lost friends because of your use of drugs?

    ○ Yes
    ○ No

11. Have you neglected your family because of your use of drugs?

    ○ Yes
    ○ No

12. Have you been in trouble at work because of your use of drugs?

    ○ Yes
    ○ No

13. Have you lost a job because of drug abuse?

    ○ Yes
    ○ No

14. Have you gotten into fights when under the influence of drugs?

    ○ Yes
    ○ No

15. Have you engaged in illegal activities in order to obtain drugs?

    ○ Yes
    ○ No

16. Have you been arrested for possession of illegal drugs?

    ○ Yes
    ○ No

17. Have you ever experienced withdrawal symptoms (felt sick) when you stopped taking drugs?

    ○ Yes
    ○ No

18. Have you had medical problems as a result of your drug use (e.g., memory loss, hepatitis, convulsions, bleeding, etc.)?

    ○ Yes
    ○ No

19. Have you gone to anyone for help for a drug problem?

    ○ Yes
    ○ No

20. Have you been involved in a treatment program especially related to drug use?

    ○ Yes
    ○ No

Score: _____

Date of Birth: _____   Age: _____

History of Substance Use

Substance:	Age of 1st Use	Age of Regular Use	Date of Last Use	Route of Administration	Frequency & Amount
Alcohol					
Cannabis					
Cocaine					
Amphetamine					
Opiates					
Sedatives					
Other:					

Stop Overthinking!
tips for better decision-making

Life is full of countless decisions, both big and small. **Overthinking** is when you devote too much time or energy trying to make the *perfect* decision, leading to anxiety and paralyzing doubt. Consider the suggestions below to tame overthinking and navigate decisions more smoothly:

Settle for "good enough" over "perfect."

The difficult truth is that you must make all decisions with only partial information. You'll never have time to consider things from all possible angles. Gathering too much information to make a "perfect" choice clouds your thinking and slows you down.

Try it out: Set limits on how long to research or analyze. Then make a decision, even if it feels imperfect.

Trust yourself over the opinions of others.

Asking for advice is helpful, but only to a point. Others may want the best for you, but have different goals or values. If you outsource your decision-making, you may lose trust in your own inner compass.

Try it out: Instead of asking someone what to do, use the conversation to clarify what feels right to you.

Distinguish between likely and unlikely outcomes.

Decision-making is agonizing if you fixate on the millions of things that *could* go wrong, but probably won't. Conserve your energy and reach clarity sooner by considering only the likely scenarios.

Try it out: Write down possible outcomes for a decision you face. Cross out any that are unlikely to happen. Then circle the two or three most likely scenarios. Keep your focus on those as you decide.

Make unimportant decisions more quickly.

Trivial decisions — like what toothbrush to buy — aren't worth your precious time and energy. If you can learn to breeze through small decisions, you'll be better equipped to take on big ones.

Try it out: When obsessing about a decision, stop and ask yourself if it will matter in a week or a month. If not, go ahead and make it quickly. Then reward yourself for upping your decision-making game!

Use your values as a roadmap.

Overthinking often happens when you rely too heavily on analysis. When it comes to big decisions, checking in with your values is a powerful way to get clarity.

Try it out: List your top five values. When indecisive, consider which option would best honor these values.

Settle for "good enough" over "perfect."

The difficult truth is that you must make all decisions with only partial information. You'll never have time to consider things from all possible angles. Gathering too much information to make a "perfect" choice clouds your thinking and slows you down.

Try it out: Set limits on how long to research or analyze. Then make a decision, even if it feels imperfect.

Trust yourself over the opinions of others.

Asking for advice is helpful, but only to a point. Others may want the best for you, but have different goals or values. If you outsource your decision-making, you may lose trust in your own inner compass.

Try it out: Instead of asking someone what to do, use the conversation to clarify what feels right to you.

Distinguish between likely and unlikely outcomes.

Decision-making is agonizing if you fixate on the millions of things that *could* go wrong, but probably won't. Conserve your energy and reach clarity sooner by considering only the likely scenarios.

Try it out: Write down possible outcomes for a decision you face. Cross out any that are unlikely to happen. Then circle the two or three most likely scenarios. Keep your focus on those as you decide.

Make unimportant decisions more quickly.

Trivial decisions — like what toothbrush to buy — aren't worth your precious time and energy. If you can learn to breeze through small decisions, you'll be better equipped to take on big ones.

Try it out: When obsessing about a decision, stop and ask yourself if it will matter in a week or a month. If not, go ahead and make it quickly. Then reward yourself for upping your decision-making game!

Use your values as a roadmap.

Overthinking often happens when you rely too heavily on analysis. When it comes to big decisions, checking in with your values is a powerful way to get clarity.

Try it out: List your top five values. When indecisive, consider which option would best honor these values.

Realize that *not* deciding is a decision.

It can be tempting to delay difficult or uncomfortable decisions. This may seem like a way of avoiding a bad outcome. But what you're really doing is allowing life to decide for you, which can make you feel passive and powerless.

Try it out: Write down the consequences of endlessly delaying a decision. What might you miss out on?

Recognize that some decisions may not feel good.

It's unrealistic to expect every decision to give you warm fuzzies. Many daily choices are likely to feel neutral, while big dilemmas can feel incredibly difficult, regardless of what you decide.

Try it out: Write down the emotion you struggle with most when making decisions. List three ways you can cope with this feeling rather than overthinking or procrastinating.

Accept that risk is unavoidable.

Every decision comes with some risk. Avoiding obviously dangerous decisions makes sense, but taking reasonable risks to move toward your goals is necessary to learn, grow, and thrive.

Try it out: When faced with a tough decision, ask if it will bring you closer to a cherished goal or value. Is the risk worth the potential reward? What would be the risk of doing nothing?

Know that every decision involves loss and compromise.

Loss is an inevitable part of decision-making. By choosing one path, you're forgoing another. If you choose to move to New York, you're choosing *not* to live in Seattle. But maybe part of you really wanted to live in Seattle. And that can be a heartbreaker.

Try it out: After making a decision, acknowledge what you had to give up, but embrace the path you chose.

Resist reversing decisions out of doubt.

You make a decision and then feel overcome by doubt. Sound familiar? It's tempting to reverse a decision to alleviate anxiety, but this rarely works. In fact, you'll probably want to reverse the reversal!

Try it out: When feeling doubt, ask if there's something truly new to consider. If not, stay the course.

OcYM globally inspires confidence, optimism, creativity, and peace through words, arts, and fashion to enhance a positive mindset towards ·life.

https://ocymbasketball.com
https://ocymglobal.com

Dedicated to Andrew and Jean.